Introducti<

The Heart of Wales Railway links Shre
the way, passes through some of Wales' mo
as being a spectacular journey, the line provides access to spienuiu wai..-g
country, and gives you the opportunity to reach the start of each route without
the use of a car. From Church Stretton in the north to the line's southern ter-
minus at Swansea these walks provide a wide range of opportunities, ranging
from town and riverside explorations to more adventurous excursions into the
mountains.

Any of these walks can be undertaken by a reasonably fit person, with
none being more than moderately challenging. Walking boots or strong shoes
are recommended for all of them, and *please* keep in mind that this is sheep
farming country – *dogs must be kept on a lead at all times (or left behind).*

The location of each walk and its station starting point is shown on the
back cover, and a summary and the length of each is given on a special chart
on the inside back cover. An *estimated* duration is also given for each walk,
but for those who enjoy fine views and like to linger over them, or to explore
the attractions visited, it is best to allow longer. If you are travelling by rail, it
is *essential* that you check the timetable, to *ensure* you have allowed sufficient
time to meet the train for your return journey. For train timetable enquiries
and tickets ring 01597 822053 or visit www.arrivatrainswales.co.uk. You can
also buy tickets on the train. Llandrindod Wells is the only manned station
between Shrewsbury and Llanelli. Visit: www.heart-of-wales.co.uk for general
information.

Each walk has a map and description which enables the route to be followed without further help, but always take account of the weather and dress
accordingly, especially if you are exploring the higher routes.

A weather forecast for the area crossed by the line can be obtained at
www.metoffice.gov.uk, or by ringing 09068 500 414 for Mid-Wales or 09068
500 409 for South Wales (charge).

Please respect local traditions, and always take special care of the envi-
ronment, so that all those who wish to enjoy the great charm and beauty of
The Heart of Wales Line, and the countryside it passes through, may continue
to do so.

This guide would not exist without the enthusiastic support of the
Heart of Wales Line Travellers Association, especially David Edwards, Roger
Baldwin, Peter Davies, Martin Loake and all the other members who have
assisted. Special thanks are also extended to Mike Wilson and the Heart of
Wales Line Forum, who got the project 'off the ground'.

Enjoy your walking!

A WALK BACK IN TIME

DESCRIPTION This station-to-station walk meanders through undulating countryside to the Acton Scott Historic Working Farm, which splendidly recreates farming life as it was at the turn of the century. The whole route is about 8½ miles long, and will take approximately 5 hours (NOT including time spent at Acton Scott).

START Craven Arms SO432830 or Church Stretton SO445935.

1 Leave Craven Arms Station from the southbound platform, walk to the main road and turn LEFT. When you reach the speed derestriction road signs, turn RIGHT along the signed path by the horse trough. Cross the footbridge and go through the kissing gate to the right. Follow the path across a field, pass through another kissing gate and turn RIGHT. Pass the 'School House' on your left and immediately turn LEFT through a gate. Walk with the hedge on your left, cross a stile and continue. Go through a gate and continue to walk ahead, now with an old hedge on your right. Continue ahead when a fence joins your route from the left. Cross a double stile and follow the path through trees, with the river below you on the left. Cross a stile into a field and continue ahead walking around trees on the left. Continue ahead, then cross a stile by a gate on the left, to follow a track under trees.

2 Pass Berrymill Cottage, go through a gate and carry on AHEAD, with a fence on your left. Go through a gate and continue on to a stile. Cross this and walk ahead. Step across a tiny stream to reach a footbridge with stiles. Cross this and turn RIGHT. Cross a stile beside a gate and continue with a fence on your left. Cross a stile beside a gate and continue, crossing the next stile by a gate, which is between houses. Now follow the lane. You soon join another lane, where you turn LEFT.

3 After about 20 yards, turn RIGHT, crossing a stile by a gate. Continue, crossing a stile by a gate, and then another stile. Now look out for a stile on your RIGHT. Cross this, walk across the field and cross the stile opposite. Walk over the footbridge and continue ahead, towards the right-hand side of a prominent house. Cross two fence stiles and walk HALF-LEFT to another fence stile.

4 Cross this and turn RIGHT along a lane. Follow the lane when it bends left, ignoring the track ahead. Continue ahead by Affcot Manor Farm, passing through a gate and, ignoring a lane off to the right, continue ahead and slightly left over a field to a stile, which you cross. **TAKE CARE in this area, as the farmer often uses thin electrified fences. Make sure you keep well clear as you duck under them, and WARN YOUR CHILDREN.** Maintain your direction, crossing the next stile, and continue to the next. Cross this and carry on ahead towards the central point of extensive farm buildings and silos. Walk along the lane between the buildings, then through two gates to join a road.

5 Carry straight on. When the road bends to the right by the red-brick house 'Ireland', continue ahead. When the fence and trees on your right end, maintain your direction over the field. Pass to the right of a hedge to reach a footbridge and a stile. Cross these and continue ahead over another large field. Cross a stile and footbridge and continue, bearing slightly LEFT to reach a gate and an old bridge. Go through the gate, carefully cross the bridge and continue, again bearing slightly LEFT to pass to the left of an isolated tree. You reach a stile in the fence to your left. Cross this, cross an old stone bridge and then the stile directly AHEAD. Walk AHEAD over the field, ignoring a stile over to the left. Head for the gap between two large clumps of trees, to reach a stile. Cross it and bear HALF-RIGHT to a fence stile beside a gate. Cross this and now walk with the fence on your left. Cross the stile in the corner of the field and turn RIGHT to follow a narrow path through trees to reach a stile. Cross this and continue diagonally across a field to reach a stile beside a gate. Cross this and turn HALF-RIGHT to walk across a small field. Cross a stile to reach the entrance to *Acton Scott*

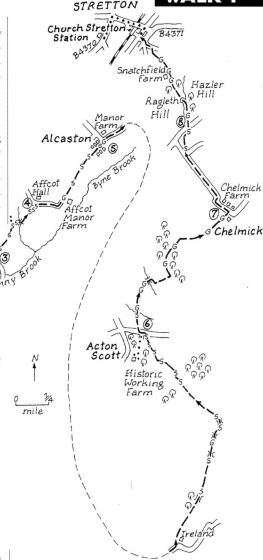

Historic Working Farm near Church Stretton. Try to make time to visit this friendly and informal museum where farming life, as it was at the turn of the century, is faithfully re-created amongst a charming collection of buildings. Open Tue-Fri 10.00-16.30. Weekends & B.Hols 10.30-17.00. Closed Mon. Café. Charge.

6 Leave Acton Scott and turn LEFT along the road, sharing the route with the 'Wagoners Wander'. Pass a gate on your right, then turn RIGHT opposite the entrance to Acton Scott Farm. Follow the track down to a stile beside a gate. Cross this and turn sharp RIGHT to go through a small wooden waymarked gate and along an old lane. When you emerge from the lane turn RIGHT to walk with the hedge on your right. Pass through a gate and continue down the path between trees. Descend to a gate, go through, cross a small bridge and walk ahead to the gate opposite. Go through the gate ahead and turn RIGHT to cross a brook and enter trees. Climb the track uphill, go through a gate and continue AHEAD, with a hedge on your right. Leave the field through the gate ahead and follow the track. Go through a gate, join a lane and turn LEFT.

7 Follow the lane as it turns right, and then left. When you reach a 'T' junction, cross the stile which faces you and cross the field, keeping to the edge of the dip to the right, as you head for the stile in the far corner. Cross this stile and cross the lane.

8 Follow the path immediately opposite the stile just crossed, now following the 'Jack Mytton Way'. Go through a gate and continue downhill, beside a stream. Soon you will step across this stream to reach a small waymarked metal gate. Go through this and continue downhill. Carry on ahead across a field, to join a fence on your left. Go through two gates and continue ahead. Go through a gate and walk between houses. You join a road and continue along the track to the right. When you join a road, turn LEFT. At the end of the road turn RIGHT, cross the road and walk to the main road. To reach Church Stretton Station, cross the main road and continue ahead.

FORTIFICATIONS OLD, & NOT QUITE SO OLD

DESCRIPTION This 5½ mile walk explores two fortifications – the stunningly romantic fortified manor house at Stokesay and the massive embankments of Norton Camp, an iron age hillfort overlooking the valley. Between the two you will pass through some splendid woodland, and there is the added bonus of a fine church, which is kept open for visitors each day. When your walk is almost over, you can relax in a friendly pub. Allow about 3½ hours for walking, as you will have to tackle a substantial, but steady, climb – and add on some extra time for visits.
START Craven Arms SO432830.

I Leave Craven Arms Station from the southbound platform and walk ahead to the main road, where you turn RIGHT. Walk beside this main road, passing three mini-roundabouts and the Craven Arms Hotel. Pass another mini-roundabout at the junction with Clun Road, and continue along Ludlow Road. Immediately after passing The Antiques Warehouse, turn RIGHT into Dodds Lane. Pass under the railway to reach a stile by a gate. Cross the stile and veer LEFT, to walk with a fence and a hedge on your left. Cross the stile in the field corner and turn LEFT, to walk again with the fence and hedge on your left. Cross a stile by a gate and maintain your direction, with the hedge on your left. You reach the railway line on your left. Walk beside it for a short distance then turn LEFT to pass underneath it in a tunnel, to be confronted with a splendid view of Stokesay Castle. Continue ahead, passing a pond to your right, to reach a gate. Go through and turn LEFT. The entrance to both The Church of St John the Baptist and Stokesay Castle is on your right. *During the 13thC wool was one of England's major exports, and the Marches were a major wool-producing area. The tenancy of Stokesay was sold to Lawrence of Ludlow, the leading wool merchant in the*

area, in 1281 and it is thought that he began building Stokesay Castle soon afterwards. It was subjected to a siege during the Civil War, and captured by the Parliamentarians. The Royalists took refuge in the church (see below), which was partially demolished during the skirmish which followed.
In 1647 the Castle was ordered to be 'slighted', or levelled, but fortunately, with the exception of the walls being lowered, little else was done. A detailed guide book is available, and this explains the features of the building in great detail. You can also use an 'audio guide', again available from the shop. Open 10.00-18.00 Apr-Sept, 10.00-18.00 or dusk Oct, 10.00-16.00 Wed-Sun Nov-Mar. Closed Christmas Eve, Christmas Day & Boxing Day. Charge. The Church of St John the Baptist was built by the Say family as the chapel for Stokesay Castle. Among the building's most appealing features are 'The Ten Commandments', with Moses and Aaron, painted on the north wall. This charming church is open every day.

2 Now continue along the lane, which bends to the right and joins the main road, where you turn RIGHT. Cross the bridge over the River Onny, then carefully cross the road (it is busy) and just beyond 'Castle View' turn LEFT. After about 25 yards, turn RIGHT to cross a stile and walk with a hedge on your left. Climb steps, cross a stile and turn RIGHT, to follow a clear path through splendid woodland.

3 Eventually you emerge at a track by a gate. Turn LEFT to walk up the track, taking the first turning to the LEFT. When the track forks, take the RIGHT fork along Rotting Lane (a rough track). At the next fork, go to the RIGHT and continue. The lane become grassy – you leave the woods through a gateway. Continue, with trees to your right. Gradually a fine view opens up to your right. Cross the stile on your RIGHT at the end of the woods and turn LEFT, to walk with the hedge on your left.

4 You reach a gate – do not go through, but turn LEFT to cross a stile and walk along a track. Go through a gate and contin-

about 120 yards to join another track, where you turn LEFT. Follow this track downhill, ignoring a footpath off to the right. When you reach a stile on your RIGHT, cross it and walk downhill, with a fence to your left. There is a fine view over Craven Arms here. Cross the stile ahead and follow the clear path across a field and down a small hollow, to a gate. Go through the gate and turn LEFT.

ue, as the track bends to the left by Campbarn. You enter trees and pass the ruins of a once-fine house on your left. Now turn LEFT in front of the ruined red-brick barn. Continue along a grassy lane, proceeding gently uphill. The lane becomes a path, and passes through brambles. Look carefully and you will notice a stile on your left. Ignore this, but about 5 yards further on turn RIGHT to follow the direction indicated by a marker post (it can tend to get a little overgrown here during late summer!). Follow the narrow path along the top of the eastern side of Norton Camp. *The massive earthworks of Norton Camp are the remains of an iron-age hill fort. The scale of the embankments is quite stunning, and the views, where there is a break in the trees, are splendid.* Continue along the path until you reach a footpath marker-post in a small hollow. Turn RIGHT here as directed. Shortly you emerge at a track in front of a pheasant-rearing enclosure. Turn RIGHT and walk for

5 Walk by Whettleton Farm to turn RIGHT, and walk along a lane. The lane bends to the right and reaches a stile by a gate. Cross the stile and turn LEFT, to walk, with the fence and hedge on your left, down to a small footbridge. Cross this and continue ahead to reach a more substantial footbridge, with white gates at each end. Cross this and continue along a lane, turning RIGHT into Newton. Turn LEFT by the pelican crossing to reach the Stokesay Castle Hotel on your left. Now turn RIGHT at the main road, by the excellent Secret Hills Discovery Centre (well worth a visit), to pass the mini-round-abouts and return to the station.

THE QUIETEST PLACES UNDER THE SUN

DESCRIPTION Passing through gentle and attractive countryside, this 6½ mile walk visits two pretty villages in the valley of the River Clun, which are celebrated in A E Housman's famous poem 'A Shropshire Lad':

> 'Clunton and Clunbury,
> Clungunford and Clun,
> Are the quietest places
> Under the Sun'

Both villages visited, Clungunford and Clunbury, have fine churches. You can, of course, undertake the walk in either direction, although starting from Hopton Heath makes for a gentler climb up the single significant hill, and allows you to enjoy the splendid pub as a reward for completing the route! Allow about 4 hours for this walk.
START Hopton Heath SO380774 or Broome SO399809.

I Leave Hopton Heath Station by climbing the steps and turn RIGHT to walk along the road towards Clungunford. When the road bends left at a junction, continue straight ahead through a gate. Veer to the right when the fence on the right ends, passing trees on your left and descending towards the River Clun to reach a footbridge. Cross this, go through a gap in the fence ahead, then turn HALF-LEFT to walk across a field to a gate. Go through and follow the lane up to the road.

2 Turn LEFT and walk along the road. When you reach a road junction, turn LEFT to walk through Clungunford, a quiet village of timbered houses and converted barns. Pass St Cuthbert's church on the right. *Most of St Cuthbert's Church dates from around 1300, although the tower was added in 1895 by E. Turner of Leicester, who also built the timber porch. The oldest part of the building is probably the north chancel chapel.* Cross the bridge over the River Clun and continue.

Housman mentioned the River Clun:
> *'In valleys of springs and rivers,*
> *By Ony and Teme and Clun,*
> *the country for easy livers,*
> *The quietest under the sun'*

Turn RIGHT by the Bird on the Rock Tea Rooms (*and you could, of course, stop for refreshment here*). Ignore the first gate on the right, but turn RIGHT at the road junction, to pass Highfield Garden on the left (*open daily, modest admission fee*). Continue along the lane, turning LEFT to pass under the Heart of Wales Line. Follow the lane.

3 Pass through a gate and continue with a fence to your left. Cross another stile and then veer to the RIGHT, away from the clear track, to reach an overgrown stile. Cross this and turn LEFT to walk along a shallow hollow to reach an old gateway (there is no gate). Go through and turn RIGHT to follow the track uphill to a gate. Go through, turn left and continue, with the hedge now on your right. Turn around to enjoy the view, then continue, going through the next gate (and ignoring the opening to the left!). When you are level with a gate on the left turn HALF-RIGHT across a field to reach a gate in the corner of the field. Cross this and continue ahead to a gate. Go through and continue, passing through a gate and walking down an old hollow lane, enjoying another splendid view, this time looking over the pretty village of Clunbury. Continue downhill, eventually reaching a metal gate. Go through and continue to the road.

4 Continue AHEAD, ignoring the turning to your right. You reach a staggered crossroads – here you should turn RIGHT to continue the walk, but you can go straight ahead to explore Clunbury and visit St Swithin's Church if you wish. *Standing in close proximity to its secular neighbours, St Swithin's Church is a bold building with a battlemented tower, probably built during the 13thC. The nave roof is a fine timber construction, typical of this area.* Continue along the lane, ignoring a signposted bridge over the river to your left. When the lane turns sharp left to cross a bridge, continue AHEAD along the lane. When the lane ends, continue

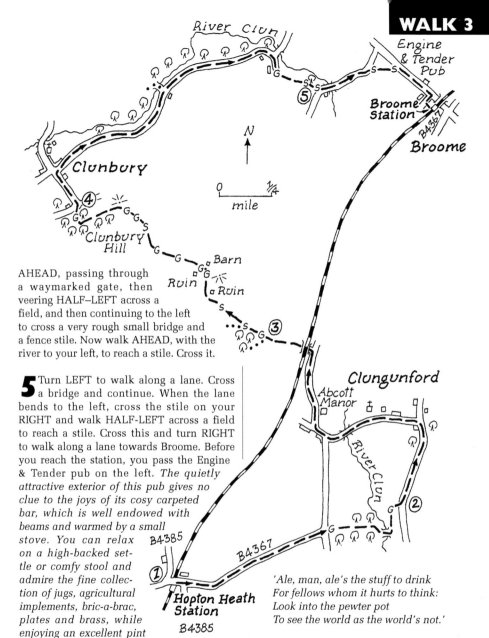

AHEAD, passing through a waymarked gate, then veering HALF–LEFT across a field, and then continuing to the left to cross a very rough small bridge and a fence stile. Now walk AHEAD, with the river to your left, to reach a stile. Cross it.

5 Turn LEFT to walk along a lane. Cross a bridge and continue. When the lane bends to the left, cross the stile on your RIGHT and walk HALF-LEFT across a field to reach a stile. Cross this and turn RIGHT to walk along a lane towards Broome. Before you reach the station, you pass the Engine & Tender pub on the left. *The quietly attractive exterior of this pub gives no clue to the joys of its cosy carpeted bar, which is well endowed with beams and warmed by a small stove. You can relax on a high-backed set-tle or comfy stool and admire the fine collec-tion of jugs, agricultural implements, bric-a-brac, plates and brass, while enjoying an excellent pint of Woods real ale, brewed in nearby Wistanstow. Indeed, they often have Wood's 'Shropshire Lad' brew on offer!* Housman wrote enthusiastically of ale in the poem:

'Ale, man, ale's the stuff to drink
For fellows whom it hurts to think:
Look into the pewter pot
To see the world as the world's not.'

Other rooms house a restaurant area, and one has some interesting railway ephem-era. Good food is served, and there is camp-ing and caravanning behind the building. Continue along the road, turning RIGHT before the railway bridge to reach Broome Station.

WALK 4

KING ARTHUR & A FOXY TALE

DESCRIPTION This moderate 5 mile walk between Knucklas and Llangunllo stations affords fine views of the tall Knucklas Viaduct, which carries the Heart of Wales Line in thirteen strides across a peaceful valley. It also visits the site of a castle associated with King Arthur, and which was later used by the Normans. You will enjoy charming countryside, visit a pretty church, and have the opportunity for refreshment in a friendly and welcoming pub. The walk can be undertaken in either direction, although these instructions read from Knucklas to Llangunllo. Allow about 3 hours.
START Knucklas SO254741 or Llangunllo SO210730.

I From Knucklas Station walk straight downhill, passing houses on the left, to reach a main road, where you turn LEFT to reach the Castle Inn, *a friendly and welcoming pub, where you will, as often as not, be greeted by the genial host amidst warm wood panelling, stone walls and slate floors. A large stove stands ready should the weather turn chilly. Real ales are served, and the bar meals are both excellently prepared and reasonably priced.* Take the fork to the right of the inn, and continue along a lane, with a stream on your right. Cross the bridge to your RIGHT and then walk up a lane to the LEFT by a telephone kiosk, with views of Knucklas Viaduct soon appearing through the hedge on your left. *Knucklas Viaduct, which strides purposefully across the valley of the Ffrwdwen Brook, was completed in August 1863. It stands 69 feet tall, and has 13 arches each with a span of 35 feet 9 inches. A fox, while being chased by the local hunt in 1925, leapt off the top of the viaduct when it found itself trapped by workmen, who were crossing from the opposite end. Whether or not it died upon landing, it was certainly finished off by the pursuing hounds. The inscription 'FOX' has apparently been carved into the lintel from which it leapt.* Continue along

the lane, ignoring a gate on the left. When the lane bends to the right, take the green lane ahead. *Cnwclas Castle, standing on Castle Hill, above Knucklas, occupies a strategic position overlooking a point where the Ffrwdwen Book joins the River Teme. The hill was originally topped with an iron-age hillfort, and was associated in legend with King Arthur and Queen Guinevere. Crowned later with a stone keep, this last fortification was begun by Ralph Mortimer and completed in 1242 by his son Roger. It was taken by Owain Glyndwr's army in 1402, during that last great flourish of Welsh independence. Now very little of the castle remains.*

2 You reach a stile on your LEFT. Cross it, walk down to the railway, **stop, look and listen, and cross the track if all is clear**. Cross the stile on the other side and turn RIGHT to walk with a fence on your right. Go through a gate and then walk diagonally LEFT down the field, towards a stream. Go through a broken gateway and cross a bridge over the stream. Continue directly ahead to a gate, go through it, and turn RIGHT.

3 Note the lane which joins from the left at Heyop, but continue for a short distance ahead for a closer look at the church. *The tiny settlement of Heyop is intimately attached to St David's Church, a striking little structure erected by J L Pearson in 1880-2, upon the foundations of an earlier building.* Now return to the road junction and turn RIGHT. Pass

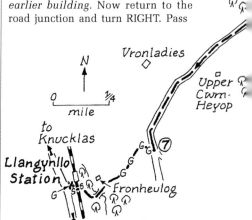

8

a farm entrance on the left and, a short way further on, go through the first gate on the RIGHT. Walk LEFT across the field to another gate, and go through to reach a second gate. Go through and turn HALF-RIGHT to head towards a small group of conifer trees and a fence corner, and continue with the fence to your left.

4 You reach a gate. Go through it and continue with the fence now on your right. Cross a stile on your RIGHT, by a house, and turn LEFT. Go through a gate, turn RIGHT, and walk steeply uphill, to reach a fence stile. Cross it, and walk ahead, just to the left of a wooden electricity pole, to reach two gates. Go through the LEFT-HAND gate, turn LEFT and walk with the hedge on your left. Go through the gateway ahead, and then through another four gates beside a little-used farmyard. Cross the two large gates on the LEFT, turn RIGHT and walk with the hedge on the right.

5 Turn RIGHT at the track to go through a gate towards the farm, then almost immediately turn very sharp LEFT down to a stile to the right of two gates. Cross the

on the way. Walk beside the buildings to go through a gate to reach a lane.

6 Turn LEFT and walk along this quiet lane. Ignore a right fork and continue. Ignore footpath signs by an entrance on the right. The lane bends to the left.

7 Just before a track forks off to the left, turn sharp RIGHT to go through a gate, directly opposite a Glyndwr's Way waymark post. Walk down to a track and turn LEFT through a gate. Walk along the track with a hedge on the left. Go through a gate beside a barn and continue ahead. Then go through another gate and continue. Veer LEFT below a farmhouse to walk down to an old footbridge over a stream. It is VERY muddy either side of the bridge, so take your time and find the driest route. Cross the bridge and follow the path up through the trees to the top. Now turn HALF-RIGHT and walk across the field towards the station. Cross the stile, stop, look and listen, and cross the railway line **if all is clear**. Cross the stile opposite and turn RIGHT. Go through gates and

stile (take care, it is loosely fixed) and walk with a hedge on your left to reach an old gate. Go through and walk AHEAD, skirting marshy ground, and then trees, on the left. Go through a gateway and continue with trees and a ravine to the left. Reach a stile, cross it and follow a green lane downhill. Go through a gate just to the right of the track and walk down to the stile at the left-hand end of farm buildings, passing through a gate

walk between houses to reach Llangunllo Station, to catch the train. *Llangunllo Station stands close to the summit of the line, which reaches a height of 980 feet just a little north of here by Llyncoch Tunnel, itself 1935 feet long. It is said that if you look down the track from Llangunllo you will notice a slight kink in the line, caused by a farmer who 'adjusted' the surveyors' pegs in order to preserve his access to a spring!*

ON THE TRAIL OF GLYNDŴR

DESCRIPTION Climbing steadily from Llangunllo Station to a height of 1640 feet this route explores the remote uplands where Glyndŵr's Way passes close to the source of the River Lugg. You will cross Beacon Hill Common, a fine expanse of land where there is the opportunity to see some of the rarer upland birds, and enjoy splendid views. The walk is 5 miles long 'station to station' if you catch a train at Llanbister Road, but you can extend the route to 8 miles by returning to your starting point along quiet lanes. Allow about 3 hours for the 'station to station' route, or 4½ hours for the circular route. There are no pubs, so bring a picnic.

START Llangunllo SO210730 or Llanbister Road SO174716.

I Leave Llangunllo Station and turn RIGHT to walk along the lane. When you reach a road junction continue AHEAD along a 'No Through Road', starting to climb gently and eventually passing 'Ferley' on your right. Go through a gate and continue along the lane. Pass Ferley Hall on your left and continue. Go through a gate and continue, then pass through another two gates to pass Upper Ferley, then take the lane ahead (don't go to the right!). You have now left the tarmac.

2 Go through a gate and turn RIGHT along a track, which continues your steady climb. Turn around to enjoy a fine view opening up behind you. Stay on the track as you pass a signpost to your right, then go through a gate and continue. Go through the next gate and then IGNORE the gate on your left.

3 Turn LEFT immediately after it, to walk over Beacon Hill Common. *This common is owned by the Crown Estate, and comprises 1889 hectares (4667 acres) of upland moor, parts of which are designated as Sites of Special Scientific Interest. There are ancient monuments: tumuli and the Short Ditch,* which is passed on this walk. Walk along the clear track, which cuts through the Short Ditch. Gradually excellent views open up to your right. You are now walking on an exposed section of Glyndŵr's Way, a National Trail which celebrates this Welsh revolutionary. When the track forks, take the LEFT fork as waymarked and continue along the green track for about 400 yards until you reach an indistinct cross-tracks.

4 You can check your position by looking over to your right, where you will see the roof of a barn about a quarter-of-a-mile away. Turn LEFT here and follow the track over a small hill. Continue ahead as the track becomes just a path, and pass to the right of a small lake. When this lake is immediately on your left, start to veer slightly left and look out for a clear track, which starts to descend into a small cwm. You will cross a marshy patch, which is in fact the source of the River Lugg (although it can dry up during the summer). Now veer LEFT to walk to the right of the river and parallel to it, staying above the gorge and following a distinct track. Gradually the river starts to head away to your left, but you stay on what is now a clear track, starting to descend *and enjoying the sweeping views ahead.* Eventually you reach a gate, which you go through to continue along a hedged track, keeping a radio mast ahead.

5 Go through the gate at the bottom and turn RIGHT. When you reach a road continue AHEAD (don't turn left), then turn LEFT at the road junction, to walk along a lane. When the lane veers to the right and just before it starts to descend, go through the angled gate on the LEFT and walk DIAGONALLY across the field. As you start to descend, walk towards the gap in the trees ahead. Ignore a gate on your left, and walk down to a gate in the hollow ahead. Go through and walk down to a gate on the RIGHT. Go through this and walk HALF-LEFT to a small footbridge. Cross this and walk slightly RIGHT to reach a stile. Cross this and you are on Llanbister Road Station. You can now catch the train, or walk back to the start along quiet lanes. (Leave the station

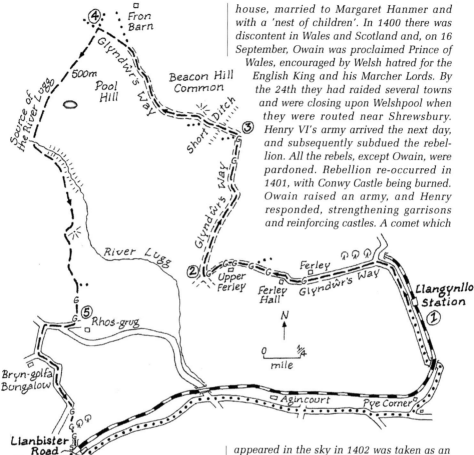

house, married to Margaret Hanmer and with a 'nest of children'. In 1400 there was discontent in Wales and Scotland and, on 16 September, Owain was proclaimed Prince of Wales, encouraged by Welsh hatred for the English King and his Marcher Lords. By the 24th they had raided several towns and were closing upon Welshpool when they were routed near Shrewsbury. Henry VI's army arrived the next day, and subsequently subdued the rebellion. All the rebels, except Owain, were pardoned. Rebellion re-occurred in 1401, with Conwy Castle being burned. Owain raised an army, and Henry responded, strengthening garrisons and reinforcing castles. A comet which

appeared in the sky in 1402 was taken as an omen, since its tail was said to point towards Wales. Owain's rebellion grew, defeating the English at Pilleth, near Knighton, at a place called Bryn Glas. Owain then moved south, and also blockaded the castles at Harlech and Caernarfon. By 1404 Owain had secured Wales, taken Harlech Castle and established a Parliament in Machynlleth. Eventually King Henry became ill, and gave Prince Henry a free hand to campaign, successfully, in Wales, turning Owain into a fugitive. In 1407 the rebellion faded through starvation and a lack of funds. By 1410 it was all over. Owain Glyndŵr faded from history, and perhaps died on the 20th September 1415 at Monnington-on-Wye, or on an exposed mountain ridge in Gwynedd. Or maybe he ended his days quietly at Pwllirch, Darowen.

and turn left. Continue ahead at the first road junction, turn left at the next, and left again at Pye Corner, to return to Llangunllo.)

Who was Owain Glyndŵr? In 1284 Edward I completed England's conquest of Wales, when Llywelyn was killed in a skirmish with English forces at Cilmeri, near Builth Wells. Owain ap Gruffydd, Owain Glyndŵr, was born around 1359, the son of Gryffydd Fychan and a descendant of the royal house of Powys. He became Squire to Henry Bolingbroke, King Richard's cousin, and during this period he would have learned his fighting skills. His military career over, he settled near Sycharth in a moated wooden

WALK 6
UN-COMMONLY GOOD WALKING

DESCRIPTION Walking from one wonderfully remote station, Llanbister Road, to another, Dolau, this 6½ mile route crosses Coxhead Bank Common and passes by the mound of Castell Cymaran (private). It is easy walking, allowing you plenty of time to enjoy a serenely peaceful part of Radnorshire. If you are feeling energetic, you can return to your staring point along narrow and quiet country lanes, lined with summer flowers, and autumn blackberries. Allow about 3½ hours for a one way walk, or about 5 hours if you walk back along the lanes to Llanbister Road. There are no pubs on this walk, so bring refreshments – you are sure to find a pleasant spot for a picnic if the weather is fine.
START Llanbister Road SO174716 or Dolau SO140671.

I Climb the steps from Llanbister Road Station, go through the gate and turn LEFT. At the road junction turn RIGHT (as signed for Dolau). Continue along the lane to reach houses at Cwm-y-gaist, and turn RIGHT by 'Cwm Islwyn'. When the tarmac ends, continue straight ahead to cross over the railway line on a wide bridge. Go through a gate and turn HALF-LEFT to walk along a shallow dip in the field. Ford a stream (there are some pipes to carefully step across if the water is high) and go through the RIGHT-HAND gate, to walk with a fence on your left. Go through a gate and continue ahead, walking beside a very fine, but overgrown, hollow green lane. Go through the gate ahead and maintain your direction over the field up to the top right-hand corner, where you join a farm track and turn RIGHT.

2 Cross a cattle-grid and turn HALF-LEFT to walk across Coxhead Bank Common. *This is a splendid expanse of land, offering fine views to the south-west. You should, of course, keep to the right-of-way across here, since the popular belief that common land is owned by the public is incorrect. Most medieval villages had several acres on the edge of the settlement set aside for the use of the villagers, but all this common land was actually privately owned, either by the Lord of the Manor, collectively by the local villagers or perhaps even by a city corporation. What is held 'in common' by certain local individuals or their families is the right to use this land. If you were such a tenant, you were known as 'a commoner', and, as such, had rights: of pasture – to graze specified livestock; of estovers – to gather and take wood (but not fell trees); in the soil – to take sand, coal or minerals; of turbary – to dig peat for fuel; and of piscary – to catch fish from ponds or streams. This extended only to that which the ground produced naturally, ie. there was no right to plant crops, and there were often seasonal limitations. Usually 'Bye Law men' were appointed annually from the tenants of the common, and it was their job to care for hedges, gates, drains and ditches.* Continue, descending gradually and keeping an infant stream to your right, then veering right to walk down to the road. During the summer the path is hidden amdst bracken up to 6 feet tall. (As an alternative you continue along the farm track until it meets a road, where you turn left.) Turn LEFT and continue ahead, ignoring a road off to the left. Pass the substantial motte and bailey of Castell Cymaran on your left. *The substantial mound and embankment of Castell Cymaran can still be seen here, and it is thought that building began around 1093, instigated by Ralph Mortimer. By 1134 it had been destroyed by Madog ab Idnerth. It was rebuilt in 1144 by Hugh Mortimer, and taken six years later by Cadwallon ap Madog. When Cadwallon died the castle was subjected to many disputes, and was taken and retaken by opposing forces. Bishop Giles Braose of Hereford and Llewelyn ap Iorwerth destroyed it in 1215, but in 1240 it was again rebuilt, and occupation certainly continued until 1360. None of the castle buildings remain. The ground is private: please do not go through the gate.* Continue along this quiet lane, passing Lower Sign farm, with its fine wooden barns, also on the left.

3 At the road junction turn LEFT. When the tarmac lane bends to the left, continue AHEAD through a signed wooden gate. Walk along the hollow lane, with the hedge on your left. Go through a gate, walking now with a fence to the right, then turn RIGHT at the far side of a field, to walk along a wide track. Go through a gate and continue ahead along a track. Pass through another gate, and then another, keeping the modern breeze-block and timber barns to the right, to follow the track to the right through Far Hall farmyard. When the track bends to the left, you leave the farmyard through a gate and then immediately turn RIGHT down a green lane.

4 Cross a bridge and go through the gate ahead to walk slightly LEFT across a field towards two gates side-by-side in the far corner. Go through the newer of the two gates and continue ahead along a track. You reach a gate ahead, with a gate to the right. Go through the gate AHEAD, leaving the track, to walk with the hedge to the right. Go through a gate and walk ahead to the far corner of the field.

5 Cross the stile and then immediately turn LEFT to cross a fence stile. Turn RIGHT to cross the railway bridge, climb the stile and turn LEFT to walk with the fence to your left. Go through a gate and continue ahead, passing through another gate, with the railway line to your left. Walk to the right of the chapel to pass through a gate to reach the road. Turn LEFT to arrive at Dolau Station.

It is hard to believe that the splendidly well-cared for Dolau Station is just a 'request only' stop, since it has fine floral decorations, a plate-layers trolley, a Victorian clock and lamp, and a splendid little waiting room containing a fascinating display of 'best-kept station' awards, historic photographs of the railway and framed poems. The station was opened in 1864, and once had a small goods and coal yard, and a signal box. By 1983 it had become very run down, prompting the formation of the Dolau Station Action Group, who are to be applauded for all the excellent work they have done.

You can now take the train from Dolau Station, or enjoy a pleasant walk along very quiet lanes back to Llanbister Road Station, by continuing along the road, with the station to your right. Take the first turning on the LEFT, and then turn LEFT again at the next road junction. Just continue along this lane to eventually return to your starting point.

Map labels: Llanbister Road Station — walk 5; to the B4356; Cwm Islwyn; ford; Cwm-y-gaist; Coxhead Bank Common; cattle grid; Cil-y-byddar; Castell Cymaran; Newhouse Farm; Lower Sign; to the A483; N; 0 — ¼ mile; Tynywain; Far Hall; Tynywain Wood; Nantywellan; Nantywylan Wood; River Aran; Chapel; Dolau Farm; King's Head Cottages; to the A488; Dolau Station; to the A483; to the A488

WALK 7
TAKING THE WATERS

DESCRIPTION The charming, spacious, elegant and genteel spa town of Llandrindod Wells grew from a few scattered cottages. Promoted by Dr Wessel Linden's treatise on the health-giving effects of 'taking the waters' in 1756, the enterprise lasted some 40 years before falling into disuse. It was the building of the railway in 1865, which fortunately coincided with a Victorian obsession with drinking mineral waters, that finally brought about the town's rapid growth. This moderate 7 mile walk explores the town, visits The Lake, St Michael's church and Cefnllys Castle, and returns via the excellent Cycle Museum. Allow about 4 hours.
START Llandrindod Wells SO059613.

When you arrive at Llandrindod Station, make sure you visit the *Signal Box Museum, which is open 11.00-12.30 & 13.30-15.00 Whitsun, Fri & Sat, Sun when there is a train service, and all week during Victorian Week, which is staged in August each year.* Now cross over the footbridge and turn LEFT. Fork RIGHT into the High Street, and go straight ahead at the roundabout to enter Rock Park & Spa. Walk ahead then fork RIGHT over the footbridge to visit the Pump Room. *One hundred years ago, during the season, you would have had to join a queue in order to take the waters, which were dispensed in The Pump Room, and were thought to have such a beneficial effect on your health. Open 09.00-13.00 & 14.00-17.00 Mon-Fri. Next door there is a fine café.* Now leave The Pump Room and walk ahead, with the stream on your left, *to visit the Chalybeate Spring, opened in 1819.* Walk back up the slope and take the tarmac path uphill to your LEFT. When you reach a path cross-roads, by a street lamp, turn LEFT. Cross the footbridge and turn RIGHT to walk through a subway under the railway, fork left and follow the path over a small bridge to reach Temple Street. Carefully cross the road, walk up the road almost opposite and continue ahead into the park, passing the skateboard ramp on your left. When you reach a road, turn RIGHT. Pass the remains of Capel Maelog on your left.

2 When you reach The Lake, turn RIGHT, to walk with the water on your left, passing the café and craft shop. *The lake was created out of a bog in 1872-3, and is overlooked by Llandrindod Wells old parish church, dating from 1291.* Turn LEFT when you reach the road and continue by the lake. Stay by the lake at the next road junction and follow the road as it bends left, until you reach the Picnic Area sign.

3 Cross the road and take the signed track on the RIGHT through trees (if you pass the Picnic Area sign on the left, you have missed the path!). The path climbs steeply uphill to steps, and continues. When the path forks, go to the RIGHT to reach a gate. Go through and continue uphill, veering LEFT below the fence. There are excellent views over the town here. Walk with the fence to your right to reach a stile. Cross it and walk towards the clubhouse on the golf course. *Please take care here, keep off the greens, watch out for golfers and if you have a dog with you, keep it on a lead.* As you approach the clubhouse turn LEFT to walk with the road to your right. Eventually you reach a stile to the left of some barns. Cross it and continue, veering right to a stile by a gate. Cross it and continue ahead to a stile by a gate. Cross this and continue ahead to another stile, which you cross. Walk uphill to a cairn and obelisk, and enjoy the views, then continue down to a stile in the field corner.

4 Cross this stile and turn LEFT to walk along a lane. Follow this lane until it becomes a track, passing organic vegetable gardens on the right. When this track veers right and ascends, cross the stile on the LEFT and follow the track, with a fence to your right. Go through a gate and walk along a clear track through woods. When the path forks, take either route to reach a kissing gate. Go through and continue to reach a road. Turn LEFT then, after about 10 yards, turn RIGHT.

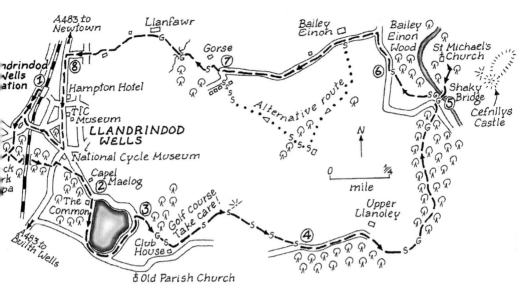

5 Go through the gate head and cross the Shaky Bridge. *There is a fine painting of it in the town museum.* Now follow the clear path to visit the church, which stands *in a wonderful setting, completely isolated in a valley. St Michael's Church is enclosed by a circular churchyard, indicating pre-Christian origins.* Now leave the churchyard and return to the Shaky Bridge, *enjoying the view of Cefnllys Hill over to your left, which is topped with the fallen remains of two castles.* Cross the bridge, go through the gate and immediately turn RIGHT to go through a kissing gate, then immediately LEFT to climb a stile. Having climbed the stile, walk diagonally uphill across a field, veering right around a hollow to reach a stile in the top corner.

6 Cross this stile and turn RIGHT along a lane. Follow the lane as it turns to the left and continue. (You can extend your walk if you turn LEFT and follow the track up the hill continuing until you reach a barn on the left. *This used to be a café visited by sweethearts on a Sunday afternoon, who would walk here to enjoy the speciality meal – egg & chips!* Take the stile on the right to return to the main route).

7 When the lane bends sharply by a large marker stone, continue ahead and slightly to the right, ignoring a track off to the left. After a short distance, turn LEFT as directed by a finger post, to the front of a house. You come to a stile, which you cross and turn RIGHT, to walk along a narrow path by a fence. Veer left with the fence, and then turn RIGHT to go through a kissing gate and cross a small stream. Now continue ahead, with a hedge on your right. Go through a kissing gate and turn LEFT along a lane. Continue, passing between houses, as the track soon becomes a lane. Cross a cattle grid to reach a road. Cross this and walk ahead down Quarry Lane.

8 Turn LEFT at the main road, and pass the Tourist Information Centre and Museum on your left, *containing a fascinating collection of relics of local interest, including a painting of the Old Shaky Bridge and a fine Speed map of the county.* Continue, to reach the National Cycle Museum, *a splendidly presented exhibition of old and new bicycles. Open 10.00-16.00 daily (Tue & Thur only Nov-Apr). Charge.* Now leave the Cycle Museum, walk up Spa Road opposite, cross the railway bridge and turn RIGHT to return to the station.

WALK 8

THE LLYWELYN MEMORIAL

DESCRIPTION Starting from the tiny village of Cilmery, where you will find a substantial memorial to Prince Llywelyn, this 8½ mile walk visits St Cannen's Church, a charming and well hidden little gem, before finding its way down to the River Wye, which tumbles over stones between wooded banks. Much of the return route follows a quiet country lane, giving splendid views over the Wye Valley. Just before you reach the station you can visit the Prince Llewelyn Inn, a splendidly unspoilt and old-fashioned pub. Allow about 5 hours for this walk.
START Cilmery SO003512.

I Walk up the lane from Cilmeri Station to the main road and turn RIGHT. Cross the road and, when you reach 'The Old Post Office', turn LEFT along the signed route. When you are behind the house, don't follow the track, but cross the stile to the right and walk diagonally across the field as directed by the waymark. When you reach the far corner, turn RIGHT to follow the track, with a stream to your left. Pass through a gap in the trees and continue with the hedge to your left. Cross a stile ahead to enter the churchyard and visit the church. *On the banks of the river Chwefri, the diminutive St Cannen's Church was founded shortly after 500 AD by Cannen, grandson of Brychan Brycheiniog, who was a Christian preacher and King of Morganwy, Gwent and Garthmadryn between about 400-450 AD. It is quite likely that Llywelyn, the last native Prince of Wales, was interred here for a while after being killed at Cefn-y-Bedd, later to become Cilmery (see below). One of the chapel walls, and the font, date from the 12thC: the nave was added in the 17thC. Although restored in 1882 by Lewis Powell of Hereford, it has retained its classic simplicity, and remains a rural gem.*

2 Leave the churchyard through the gate and walk along the lane. Turn LEFT at the junction and continue. Cross the cattle grid, passing a bridge on your left, to reach a ford. *This ford may well have been in use since Roman times, when it was on the route of a road associated with Sarn Helen.* Cross the stream and continue, passing through a gate into the yard of Neuadd-rhos-Fer farm. Exit through the gate opposite and follow the track until you reach two gates. Go through the RIGHT-HAND gate and follow the track. When you are facing a bridge under the railway, turn LEFT to walk with the railway to your right.

3 Go through a gate by Rhosferig-fawr and immediately turn RIGHT. Cross the stile and walk with the fence on your left. Ignore the stile ahead and turn RIGHT to walk down the field, beside an old, and obstructed, sunken lane. Cross the stile ahead and continue. Go through a gate on your LEFT and walk by Rhosferig-fach. Continue along the lane for about 50 yards, then cross the stile on your RIGHT, and walk HALF-LEFT across the field. You reach a stile by the railway. Cross this, descend steps and **CAREFULLY cross the track, ensuring that there are no trains approaching**. Follow the path through trees and cross the stile. Now walk HALF-LEFT across the field to a break in fence. Negotiate this break, cross the track and climb the break in the fence opposite. Continue, maintaining your direction. Pass through a short stand of conifers and cross the stile. Turn RIGHT and continue, passing an isolated oak tree to reach a stile ahead.

4 Climb this stile and continue ahead, to cross a well-hidden stile to your RIGHT. Negotiate another stile and continue, with a fence on your right (and a duckpond on your left). Cross a further stile and carry on, now with a fence to your right. When you reach a stile on your RIGHT, cross it and maintain your direction on a path through woods. The path winds beneath trees to eventually reach a stile by a gate. Cross this and follow the clear track over the golf course. When you reach the road, turn LEFT.

5 When the road bends to the left, ignore the footbridge on the right but turn RIGHT through a kissing gate and walk with

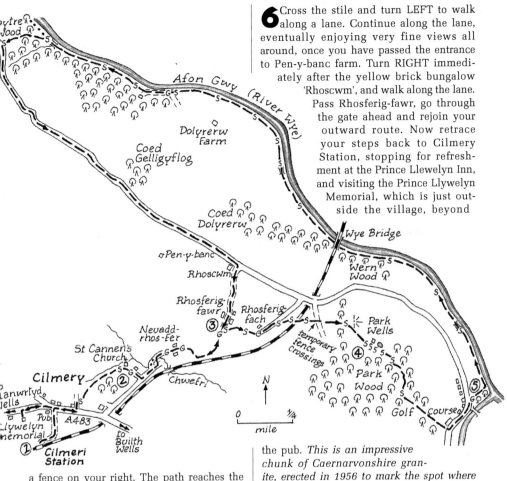

6 Cross the stile and turn LEFT to walk along a lane. Continue along the lane, eventually enjoying very fine views all around, once you have passed the entrance to Pen-y-banc farm. Turn RIGHT immediately after the yellow brick bungalow 'Rhoscwm', and walk along the lane. Pass Rhosferig-fawr, go through the gate ahead and rejoin your outward route. Now retrace your steps back to Cilmery Station, stopping for refreshment at the Prince Llewelyn Inn, and visiting the Prince Llywelyn Memorial, which is just outside the village, beyond

a fence on your right. The path reaches the riverside and turns LEFT. You then follow the path with the river to your right. You cross three stiles before passing under a railway bridge. Crossing a further five stiles brings you to a stile immediately before a gate. Cross the stile, go through the gate (which is beside a cattle grid) and follow the track. Stay beside the river when the track bends away to the left, up to an exotic wooden riverside retreat. Pass through the garden and cross a stile. Continue, crossing another stile under trees. When you reach a footbridge followed by a stile, cross them both then turn LEFT to follow a distinct track uphill. At the top of the steep slope maintain your direction across a field to reach a stile.

the pub. *This is an impressive chunk of Caernarvonshire granite, erected in 1956 to mark the spot where Llywelyn, the last native Prince of Wales, was killed. In 1246 he succeeded David, and rebelled against the English in 1282. Beaten, he became a fugitive and initially avoided capture by hiding in Aberedw rocks. He also managed to hoodwink his pursuers by having his horse shod with the horseshoes back-to-front! Llywelyn was eventually taken and killed on the 11th of December 1282 at Cefn-y-Bedd (later Cilmery) by Adam de Francton. His head was sent to London, but his body may have been interred for a while at St Cannen's Church, before being taken to Abbey Cwm-hir. The thirteen oaks which surround the monolith commemorate the thirteen old counties of Wales.*

WALK 9
LLANGAMMARCH WELLS & GARTH

DESCRIPTION This 6 mile walk makes a worth-while circuit encompassing the stations both at Garth and Llangammarch Wells. You will enjoy splendid views of the Eppynt, a vast upland area which has been used by the army since World War II for training, the equally bare but infinitely more peaceful hills to the north, the pleasant valley of the Irfon, remote woodlands and the small spa town of Llangammarch Wells. This circuit should take about 3 hours to complete, although you can just walk station to station either to the north or south of the river. There is a fine pub in Llangammarch Wells, where you can spend some time if you are waiting for a train.

START Either Garth SN954495 or Llangammarch Wells SN936473

I Leave the station at Garth and walk along the road, passing a 20mph section and the school to reach the main road. Turn LEFT. Walk though the village until you reach a fork in the road. Take the LEFT fork but almost immediately look over to your right for a small brown telephone exchange building. Follow the signed bridleway which leaves the road to the left of this. When you reach a waymarked gate, go through and continue ahead. Pass through a second waymarked gateway and continue ahead, gently climbing. The track now affords fine views to your right. Leaving a stand of conifers away to your left you pass through a small metal gate as the track swings gently to the right. You now descend to a gate, which you go through and carry on, now along the edge of a field with a fence to your right.

2 Go through a gateway by an old railway-wagon shed, the ruins of Treflys, and a radio mast, and continue ahead along a wide fenced track. Go through a metal gate and continue ahead, enjoying excellent views both to the north and south. You pass through another metal gate to enter a tree-lined section of this wide bridleway. Go through a metal gate and continue ahead. The track begins to gently descend

as you pass through another gate, and then another, passing a disused quarry. At the next gate, which you pass through, you catch a glimpse of the farm buildings of Llwynbrain to the right as your gentle descent continues between trees. As you go through another gate this descent begins to steepen, with the track now being made muddy by the appearance of a stream. Soon you are negotiating very deep ruts, so take care. Pass through a gate where a stream joins the track from the right and carry on ahead to finally pass through a gate to join a tarmac farm road and, maintaining your direction, you cross a bridge over the Afon Cammarch to reach a minor road.

3 Turn LEFT and walk along the road, ignoring a road which leaves to the right. As you climb this hill a strategically placed seat prompts you to turn around for a moment to enjoy the view to the north-west. Continue along the road to descend towards the village, crossing the Afon Cammarch on a bridge overlooked by St Cadmarch's Church, up on a rise to your left.

4 You pass what was once the Cammarch Hotel to your right and walk under the railway, with the station to your left. The road crosses over the Irfon and, on your LEFT, you will see a gate giving access to the riverside path. Go through this gate to walk with the water to your left (after having visited the village, if you wish). Go through a metal gate beside a disused kissing gate and carry on ahead. Pass through another metal gate, cross a tiny footbridge to reach another gate, which you go through and continue. The river narrows slightly and tumbles over rocks as you reach another gate, which you pass through. Go through yet another gate and continue, crossing a footbridge and passing through another gate before veering right through trees, with the old Pump House ahead, by the river. The Lake Hotel can be seen up to your left as you pass through a gate to reach the road.

5 Turn LEFT to walk along the road, passing the Lake Hotel and Restaurant to your left and the Golf House up to your right. The road climbs quite steeply, passing a small golf course to the left. When the road swings to the left, cross a stile on the left and continue as directed by the waymark post. You are now walking diagonally across a field: when you reach a fence corner

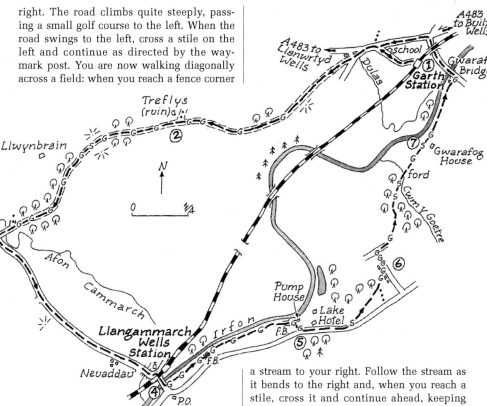

continue beyond this, following a straggly line of trees (the remains of a hedge) to turn LEFT through what was once a gateway and then, after enjoying the fine view ahead, veer RIGHT to walk towards a metal gate between houses. Go through the gate and continue ahead to another gate.

6 Go through this gate and turn LEFT, to enter a farmyard through a gate. Walk across the yard to leave it by a gate on the opposite side, and carry on ahead between sheds to reach two gates. Go through the RIGHT-hand gate to follow an obvious track. Carry on ahead, keeping the fence to your left, until you reach a gate on the LEFT. Go through this and walk downhill, with the course of a stream to your left. As you enter sparse woods look for a waymark post, which directs you ahead, now with the course of

a stream to your right. Follow the stream as it bends to the right and, when you reach a stile, cross it and continue ahead, keeping Cwm y Goetre to your right. A waymark on a tree confirms your route. You descend to stile, which you cross and continue ahead, to carefully ford the stream, picking your way where the water is shallow. Carry on, with the stream swinging away and leaving to your left. Ignore a gateway on your left and continue ahead, with the fence to your left. Pass through the remains of a gateway and continue.

7 When the track swings right by Gwarafog House, continue ahead to cross a stile, and carry on ahead. Leave the garden through a metal gate and carry on ahead with the river way down to your left. Join the road through a gateway to the right of a white wooden house and turn LEFT. Cross the bridge, walk under the railway bridge to reach the main road, where you turn LEFT. Continue along the road, soon turning LEFT to return to the station.

19

AS HIGH AS A KITE

DESCRIPTION This is an interesting 5½ mile walk with great views. The walk initially follows the valley floor and continues alongside the Afon Irfon passing below the kite feeding area and Victoria Wells towards Llanwrtyd Church. It then climbs steadily, after a short section of road walking, into the forest. You then turn abruptly to exit this to walk down by the side of the Nant Cerdin. As you climb above the Nant Cerdin there are some lovely views of the rolling countryside. **Do not attempt this walk after heavy rain, as the route involves fording the Nant Cerdin.** Allow 3 hours **START** Llanwrtyd Wells SN883464.

I Leave the station, and turn left along Station Road. When this joins Irfon Terrace, maintain your direction to reach the town centre, passing the Tourist Information and Kite Centre on your left. Turn right and walk along Dolecoed Road. Turn left and walk on the river side of the Dol-y-Coed Hotel. *This was formally a farmhouse prominent in the development of the spa trade.* Continue through a gate at the upstream end of the hotel and turn left down a path and through a gate. Ignore the track ahead. *The red kite feeding station is nearby. A local name for this spectacular hunter-scavenger, which can achieve a wing-span of almost 2 metres, is 'boda wennol', or swallow buzzard, a fitting description for such a spectacular bird, which can soar for hours with scarcely a wing beat. The longevity of the kite, if it can survive its first hazardous year, is remarkable – the oldest ringed kite recorded died at the age of 24 years. Kite feeding takes place here daily at 15.00 in summer, 14.00 in winter (www.gigrin.co.uk).* Follow the path on the bank of the Irfon to cross a footbridge that has a gate at the start and finish. At the far side turn right and follow the track as it veers left away from the river into a field. Go half left across this to a gate in the top corner. Go through this and follow the path up

to join the road opposite the entrance to the Victoria Wells Log Cabin Motel. Turn right down the road and follow it until the tarmac ends. Go straight ahead. Climb over a stile left of a gate and follow a grassy track keeping to the right of conifers to a stile right of a gate. Climb over the stile and curve leftwards to climb over another stile to join a track. Turn right and follow this track that becomes a tarmac road leading back to Llanwrtyd.

2 Turn right in front of the church and cross the bridge over the Afon Irfon. *The Church of St David's is a pretty building standing in a fine situation, built on the site of an earlier church founded by St David around 530 AD. Wales' most celebrated composer of hymns, William Williams, was curate here from 1740-43, and his portrait hangs on the south wall. His grave can be visited at St Mary's, near Llandovery. A Celtic cross, which can be seen near the font, may date from the founding of the church. In winter the building is warmed by a stove manufactured by Gurney's Warming & Ventilating Co.* Continue along the road until just past a row of terraced cottages. Turn sharp left – signed to Alltwineu. Continue up this narrow road to a 'Y' junction. Go left (right goes to Kilsby) through a gate. Continue up the narrow road and go right at the next fork. Walk over a cattle grid continuing up the narrow steep road and through a gate. Continue up to two more. Pass through the right hand one indicated by a wamark, and follow the rough track to where it ends close to a finger post. Continue straight ahead on a path and enter the forest through a gate.

3 Follow the track as it descends to a main forest road. Cross over this slightly leftwards and walk down a narrow track. Cross a stream and follow the track up to where it levels. Keep walking ahead until a short steep descent leads to the Nant Cerin. Cross this. In high water this may be impassable. Turn right immediately after crossing and follow the path that often doubles for a stream! Pass to the right of a marker post and keep following the path to join a track. Turn right and follow it, ignoring a fork to the left. Walk along to where a track goes right. Continue straight ahead over a cattle grid. Follow the level track to the next cattle grid.

4 Turn right just before this and go up to an isolated bridle gate. Pass this to the left and follow a steep grassy path trending left up the hill to join a fence. Keep this to your left and continue up the hill passing a gate in the fence on your left. Continue ahead still with the fence to your left and through a gate. Cross a boggy section and through another gate. After crossing a small stream join a

track. Go right along this until it swings to the right. Go straight ahead here through a wooden field gate. Keeping the fence to your left follow a sunken grassy path to another gate which is passed through to join a track. Turn right and go through a wooden gate 20 metres further. Keeping the house to your right follow the track and go through another gate at the end of the buildings. Continue ahead along a muddy track between trees to another gate. Go through this and another on the left where the track bends left. Follow this with trees to your right and a fence to your left. When the track enters a field turn right. Follow a line of trees on your right and where they end go through a rickety iron gate. Follow a grassy track across a field keeping above a small plantation. Where this ends go through a waymarked gate. Keep following the track to the ruins of Ffos-y-Fign. A track goes down between them. Cross over this track and go slightly left down a field to the far left hand corner to join a track just before a gate. Go through the gate and follow the track down through another gate. Walk through the farm to a gate at the end of the buildings. Follow the track down passing a pond and a large house to join the road, where you turn left to walk back to the station.

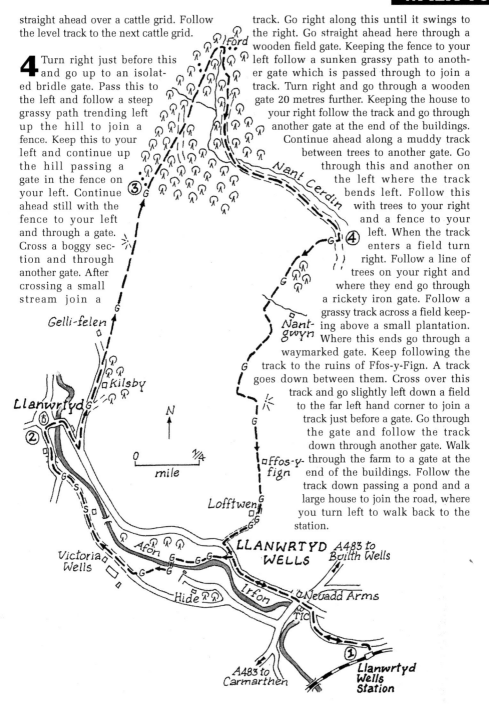

21

WALK 11

BENEATH CYNGHORDY VIADUCT

DESCRIPTION This 2¾ mile walk starts off by crossing the 'Heart of Wales' railway line before continuing across farmland. It then descends to the valley floor and continues beneath the finely constructed Cynghordy Viaduct. Continuing, the walk follows a very quiet road back to the start. It is possible to extend the walk but this includes a section of narrow and very busy main road and is not recommended. Allow 1½ hours..

START Cynghordy SN802406. Although there is limited parking alongside the track it is best not to park close to the junction with it. PLEASE DO NOT block the track as this is the access road to the station for rail users.

I Walk up towards the station. Just before reaching it turn left up to a level crossing. Climb over the stile listen for trains. If all is clear cross over and climb over a stile on the far side. Follow the track up to a way marker on your left just before the track bends right to Dildre. Go straight ahead as indicated, to the left of a huge shed, through the gate and walk up and across the field by a line of trees up to your right. Continue through a gateway. Interesting this, there is no gate and the right gate post has a fence attached to it but not the left! Walk down the field half left to a gate. Go through the gate and down the track for 20 metres. Turn sharp left to pass through a very rickety iron gate. Bear right and cross a footbridge into a field – all this is very overgrown. Walk up the field with the fence on your right to a stile at the top corner right hand corner. Go over this stile to join a track

2 Cross the track and walk diagonally right across the quite swampy field to a hidden gate with waymark, just to the right of the left hand top corner of the field. Go through the gate, cross the stream and walk up to your right on a poor track keeping the fence to your right to a marker post. Continue ahead across boggy ground to a gap in the fence. Turn left before the gap and walk up the field with the fence to your right, *where good views unfold as height is gained.* At the top of the field there is a gate. Go through this and walk between fences. This is quite awkward due to the tall sedges and grass but continue to a rusting gate. Go through this and walk down the field and through the next gate still continuing down to reach a waymarked stile on your right. Climb over the stile to enter the grounds of Pen Lan. Bear right to cross another stile and walk along the boundary of the property to your left to join a track. Follow this track down crossing over the Afon Bran before going through a gate to join the road.

3 Turn right along the road and walk beneath the superb Cynghordy Viaduct. Continue along the road passing a chapel on your left just beyond the viaduct to a bridge over the river. A track goes off left before the bridge but you will walk over the bridge and follow this quiet and quite pretty road going straight on at a 'T' junction back into Cynghordy.

*Cynghordy Station This station was opened in 1899, and a passing loop was installed in 1929. The small goods yard was removed in 1964, and the line was 'singled' a year later. Until 1995 Cynghordy sported a splendid station shelter dated 1892 – this has now been replaced with a modern and functional building. **Cynghordy Viaduct** is a sturdy and elegant structure, 846 feet long and over 100 feet above the ground at its highest point. It has 18 arches, each with a span of 102 feet. The first contractors built unsound foundations, which subsequently had to be replaced. The estimated building cost was £15,610 11s 11p – exactly (£1,234,135.30 at today's prices). The summit of the line at Sugar Loaf is 820 feet above sea level, and the tunnel is 2998 feet long. Construction was difficult, as large basins of water and unstable rock had to be dealt with. Building the line in this area was fraught with difficulties and delays – opening, originally planned for 1862, finally happened in 1868.*

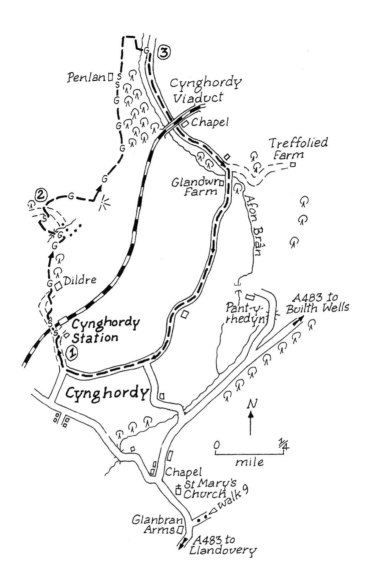

About the author, David Perrott . . .

Having moved with his wife Morag to Machynlleth from London over thirty years ago, his love of Wales remains as strong now as it was then. The founder of *Kittiwake Books*, he enjoys walking and cycling in any part of Wales. He has recently written the National Trail guide to *Glyndŵr's Way*, plus several other books and magazine articles.

WALK 12

A WALK IN 'WILD WALES'

DESCRIPTION George Borrow, author, traveller and charming eccentric, wrote his book 'Wild Wales' in 1854, recording a journey he made, on foot, through Wales. This moderate 3 mile walk visits the Castle Inn, Llandovery, where he stayed, and gives you a taste of the journey he made, as well as a splendid stroll beside the Tywi. The very many kissing gates make this an ideal walk for loved ones as the gates only open after kisses are made (!) Allow 2 kisses per gate! and about 1½ hours for the walk.
START Llandovery SN763345.

I From the station walk into the town centre, turning left to pass the Castle Hotel. *The great traveller George Borrow stayed on his journey through Wales on the 9th November 1854. He recounted the story of his journey in the very readable 'Wild Wales'.* Continue along the main road passing the Tourist Information Centre to reach the road bridge spanning the Afon Bran. Turn left along a path by the side of the terraced houses. Continue along the narrow tarmac path, with the houses to your left, to a kissing gate at its end. Bear right along the track with the river on your right to a path going off to the left below the next gate. DO NOT go through the gate. Follow the path with houses to your left and fence to your right. At a stile on your right turn left – do not go over the stile – to reach a road. Turn right and follow it to a marker post. Follow the path to the right and walk along to a gate. Walk through this and pass to the right of a play area. Keep on this tarmac path to another gate. Go through this to join the A483.

2 Carefully cross the busy road and follow the minor road quite steeply uphill to St. Mary's Church. Opposite the church on the other side of the road is a stile and a marker post. Cross the stile and head straight down the field to a hedge on your left. Continue to cross another stile and a further one 25 yards away. Walk up steps to the railway line. Cross over making sure there are no trains and walk down steps on the far side to a stile. Climb over this and go slightly left to another, easily seen some 200 yards away. Cross over and continue walking straight ahead and away from a tiny stream on your left to yet another stile. Go over this and turn right to a gate. DO NOT go through this but walk down to your left for 10 yards to a way-marked stile.

3 Step over the stile and follow the path alongside the stream on your left. Cross three short sections of boardwalk. Keep following the stream and fence to a footbridge, where there is a waymark. Cross this and go over a stile to your left. Cross another footbridge 30 yards further on. Turn right, keeping the trees to your right, along the edge of the field towards the obvious gate. Cross the waymarked stile to the left. Go left with a fence and trees to your left and walk up to a marker post. Follow the track, ignoring the one going off to the left. Keep walking along the track to a stile by a waymarked gate. Cross this and walk down the track for 50 yards to cross a stile on your left. Walk down the grassy path to yet another stile. Go over this to join a farm track. Go straight across this and go over another waymarked stile to join a tarmac road. Turn left then almost immediately right. Walk up to Pont Dolauhirion.

4 Do not walk over the bridge but turn down left to cross a stile. Follow the bank of the Afon Tywi through 3 kissing gates. After passing through the third gate, situated above small rapids, follow the edge of the field round to another kissing gate on your right. Go through this and walk up a narrow path to the left of a stream. The path ends at a kissing gate by a narrow road. Follow the road and walk up to the stone bridge seen ahead with a wooden footbridge immediately beyond. Cross the footbridge and pass through another kissing gate. Keep to the edge of the field, with a hedge on your right at first then a stone wall to, yes, another kissing gate. Go through this to join a narrow tarmac road. Cross straight over to go through another kissing gate. Turn right and walk along the edge of the field with a fence and farm buildings to your right to the familiar sight of a kissing gate. If your lips are not sore you will pass through this too and bearing right will lead you to a corrugated iron shed. Go through another kissing gate to the right of the shed and continue walking between fences to a stile by a gate. Climb over the stile and ignoring the gates to your left continue straight ahead passing through two more kissing gates. After the second one follow the path between the hedge on your left and a fence to your right to a final kiss at the last kissing gate. Go through to join the A40 and turn left back to the station.

*L*landovery *is a medieval town and borough receiving its charter in 1485 from Richard III. The famous Rhys Pritchard 1579–1644 was vicar of Llandovery who is particularly remembered for being the author of 'Ganwyll y Cymry' – The Welshman's Candle – a popular devotional work written in Welsh. Llandovery College was founded in the early part of the 19th century. Llandovery takes its name from the least worthy and very insignificant of the rivers that surround the town. Called the Nant Bawddwr – dirty water – it was diverted in 1836 through an arched culvert above which the street above paved. The Town Hall was built in 1858. The actual council Chamber was situated directly above an open arcaded market. The former Market Hall, built in the 1840s, has been renovated and now houses a craft centre atop of which is the town clock. At one time there was a tradition of clock making in the town. Information on the Castle can be found on the information board below it in the car park.*

*P*ont Dolauhirion *was mentioned as the 'Bridge at Dolhir' in 1396. This was a timber structure and the bridge you see today was built in 1773. It has a span of 30 yards and cost £800 to build. The designer was William Edwards, a minister, stone mason and a self-taught architect. He had become world famous for the bridge he had built at Pontypridd in 1750.*

THE THREE CASTLES WALK

DESCRIPTION This short and easy 4 mile walk from Llandeilo will introduce you to the delights of both the Old and New Dinefwr Castles, as well visiting the Castle Inn for a meal and a pint or two of real ale. The walk will take about 2½ hours, but you must add plenty of visiting time.

START Llandeilo SN633226.

I Leave Llandeilo Station by walking up the steps and following the brick-laid path. When you reach the road, turn LEFT and walk gently uphill along Heol Alan. You arrive at the main road, where you turn LEFT to walk into the town. Ignore the sign indicating Parc Dinefwr to your right, and carry on along the main street. Just by the zebra crossing you reach The Castle Inn on your left. *Just beyond The Castle Inn, up an alleyway by Fountain Fine Art, is a fine old chapel building, the gift of Thomas Jones of Llellygariad for 1000 years (sic). It was erected in 1788, and subsequently altered.* Continue along the main street, passing St Teilo's Church to your left. Continue down the hill, keeping to the right-hand side of the road. Turn RIGHT before the bridge and walk with the Afon Tywi on your left.

2 You come to two gates side by side. Go through the kissing gate on the RIGHT and follow the track. *Castle Woods encompass 60 acres of ancient woodland, where you should look out for great, lesser spotted, and green woodpecker, tree creeper, goldcrest, jay, magpie, sparrow-hawk, peregrine falcon, tawny owl, pied flycatcher, and redstart. The Trust also runs the Llandyfeisant Church Visitor Centre, passed on this route, and which is open weekends Easter-Oct.* When the path forks by a notice-board, go LEFT to reach the church. Follow the path around the church and go down to a gate. Go through this and turn up to your right for 10 yards to another gate, and go through. You are now on National Trust property. Walk beside the fence on your left. Go through a gate, which is shortly followed by another gate to your left. Go through and follow the path uphill through woodland. Go through a kissing gate and walk along a track, with the fence to your left. When you reach a kissing gate on your LEFT, go through and follow the path into the woods. Eventually you reach a junction with a prominent track, where you turn LEFT. You now climb steadily up to Old Dinefwr Castle. *Used as a hill fort by the Romans, the first recorded mention of this castle is in the Book of Llandaff, which refers to the site in the 7thC. It was almost certainly built around 850 AD by Rhodri Fawr in response to Viking incursions. On his death Rhodri split Wales into three kingdoms. The southern kingdom, Deheubarth, was controlled from here. By 950 Hywel Dda, Wales' most renowned leader, was based here, and Dinefwr flourished at this time. But when the Normans continued their invasion into Wales in 1067, Dinefwr's influence waned, until Rhys ap Gruffydd, new Lord of Dinefwr, began his struggle for Welsh independence in 1135, upon the death of Henry I. With others he regained independence, along with most of the land lost to the Normans. It is worth noting that Rhys was a great patron of the arts, who staged the first National Eisteddfod at Cardigan Castle in 1176. Upon his death in 1197 his sons struggled for his lands, and eventually Rhys Grug emerged with the controlling hand. He burnt the town of Swansea, took control of other castles and was eventually killed, fittingly it seems, in battle. The great Welsh Prince Llewelyn ap Iorwerth then came to power, and turned his attentions to Dinefwr. Following Llewelyn's death in 1240 there followed various changes in ownership until, in 1277, Edward I began his march into Wales, and captured Dinefwr. It was never to be returned to the Welsh. It withstood Owain Glyndwr's rebellion in 1403, and was finally abandoned by the Rhys family around 1600. The Summer House, or Belvedere, was built on top of the keep in 1660. The castle has only fairly recently been restored, and is now open.*

26

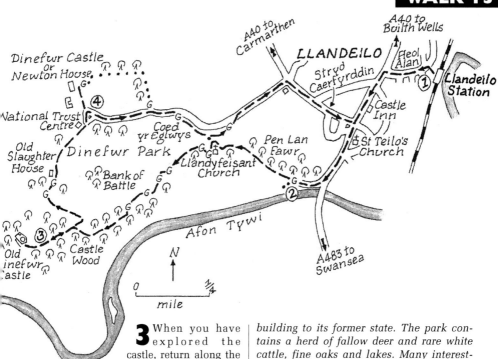

3 When you have explored the castle, return along the path, passing the junction then turning left to reach a kissing-gate below a red-roofed house. Go through, following a lane, and ignore another kissing gate to your right. Go through the gate ahead and continue along the lane. Cross a cattle grid to reach the National Trust Information Centre and Shop, *where you can purchase tickets to visit the new Castle, and watch a short introductory video. Access is gained just beyond the shop. Deriving its name from the new town established in the area by Edward I in 1298, New Dinefwr Castle or Newton House is thought to date from 1603, although there had been a 'Newton House' in these parts since about 1430. The present building was periodically altered and extended, and the grounds were inspected by the landscape architect Capability Brown in 1775, although his ideas were probably never executed. Used during the Second World War as a Casualty Clearing Station, the house, after being sold by Lord Dinefwr in the late 1970s, fell into disrepair, and was finally taken over by The National Trust in 1990. They have done their usual excellent work, restoring much of the* building to its former state. The park contains a herd of fallow deer and rare white cattle, fine oaks and lakes. Many interesting minor outbuildings surround the house. Open 11.00-17.00 Thur-Mon. Charge.

4 Now leave the house by taking the main approach road – or if you wish you can walk around the edge of the park in front of the building – this path joins the approach road further down. Follow the main approach road and, when you reach a gate on your RIGHT, go through to follow a shady path. When you reach a signpost indicating Llandyfeisant Church, turn LEFT to walk steeply uphill on a stepped path through woods. Go through a gate and continue AHEAD to reach the main road. Turn RIGHT to walk back into the town, passing the Old Market Hall on your left. Turn LEFT at the main road, to reach the Castle Inn on your right. *A very comfortable and friendly pub, with a timber lined and tiled bar, leading to other equally pleasant rooms. The food is good and they offer a wide range of real ales* Now continue until you reach Heol Alan, where you turn RIGHT to return to the station.

ONE FOR THE BIRDS

DESCRIPTION This easy 6½ mile walk between Pontarddulais and Bynea stations takes you over level ground beside the lower reaches of the Afon Llwchwr, once overshadowed by a steelworks and a colliery either side of the river at Bynea, but now splendid bird-watching country. Allow about 4 hours, wear waterproof footware, and bring your binoculars!

IMPORTANT NOTE The path by the M4 motorway bridge can become flooded at certain high tides, so please ensure that you check the time of high tide before embarking upon this walk. This information can be found in newspapers such as *The Western Mail*. BBC Wales also give high water times for the following day for the south-Wales coast at *approximately 18.50, Monday to Friday*.

START Pontarddulais SN588040 or Bynea SS550991.

I From Pontarddulais Station walk to the main road and turn LEFT. *The Gwyn Hotel, opposite the station, is a comfortable riverside pub.* When the road forks, go RIGHT (to the right of the telephone box). When you reach the Farmers Arms on the right, turn RIGHT, and then fork LEFT along Coed Bach. At the end of the road enter Coed Bach Park, and take the main path, to the right. When the path bends to the right, carry on ahead, along a grassy bank between two football pitches to reach a path. Follow this to the right, around the wire fence of the rugby pitch. The path crosses the now dismantled line of an old railway track to reach two stiles.

2 Cross the wooden stile (on the right) and walk as directed by a waymark to another stile. Cross this stile and follow the path to the left. Negotiate a muddy patch and take the wooden walkway over the field. Turn LEFT to arrive at a bridge. Cross this, pass through the gate and walk with the river on your right. Cross the next stile (20 yards from

the bank), cross the bridge, walk through the gate and resume along the path by the river. When the path leaves the river, follow it and head towards an abandoned farm. Go through the gate and continue left along the track towards the motorway.

3 You pass under the motorway, then cross a stile and follow the track as it at first bends to the left, and then to the right. Walk under the railway and continue ahead. Cross the bridge over the stream by Castell-du, turn RIGHT and climb a stile. Follow the distinct track, which bends to the left and becomes a path, with the estuary over to the right. Cross a stile and continue ahead, crossing a stream in a gully to negotiate another stile, and then walk with the fence on your right. When the fence curves away to the right, continue ahead over a boggy patch to arrive at a stile. Cross it, and the one immediately after, and carry on ahead. *The Llwchwr Estuary is a splendid place to watch birds, although you will certainly see a far greater variety during the autumn and winter. During the summer you should watch out for greenshank, which nest in north-west Scotland but move south during late summer to feed around the estuary, and little egrets, which can often be seen under the arches of the bridges: they winter south of the Mediterranean. During autumn and winter the estuary comes into its own, supporting large numbers of shelduck, widgeon, teal, mallard, oyster catcher and lapwing.* Carefully climb a tall stone step stile, which can be well hidden during the summer – look for the break in the hedge – and continue veering slightly left to a second stone stile. Cross this and continue ahead. Negotiate another stone stile, and continue ahead to a wooden stile. Climb it, cross a bridge and go across the lane.

4 Climb the stile opposite and to the left. Veer half-LEFT towards the far side of the field. When you reach a rickety, pig-wire fence corner, veer right and walk to the top corner of the field. Push through a patch of brambles to reach a stile. Cross it and the bridge and turn LEFT, to walk with a hedge on your left. *There are clumps of scarlet pimpernel and iris here in season.* You reach a kissing gate on the left. Go through it and then veer to the right. When you reach a stile by a gate, cross it and walk with a hedge on the right. When you come to a kissing-gate beyond a track, go through it and continue ahead to another stile beside a field gate. Continue, with a fence to the right, to a stile in the corner, 5 yards to the right of a field gate. Go through and walk along the track. Another track joins from the left, but you continue ahead. Go over a stile beside a gate by a house to reach a lane, which you cross.

5 Climb the stile opposite and continue, veering a little to the left, to reach a kissing gate. Go through this and continue ahead, with trees to your left. Reach a stile beside a fixed old metal gate, cross it and carry on along the path. Cross the next stile and continue ahead to cross the subsequent stile. Now follow the track, crossing a stile to the road and walking up to the left.

6 Go through the gateway and turn RIGHT along a lane. Follow this lane (ignoring signposts pointing left) until you

you reach the decoratively arranged railway sleepers, to arrive at the edge of the estuary. Continue along the path with the water and sands to your right. Leave the park through a gate, passing a small group of factory buildings on your right. Continue along the road, to emerge by the bridge.

7 Cross the river via the road bridge beside the railway *viaduct. This was built entirely of timber, by Isambard Kingdom Brunel, in 1852.* At the far end of the road bridge, turn RIGHT, descending steps, and continue ahead towards the INA Bearing Company. Turn LEFT at the end of the road, and continue, passing The Lewis Arms on your right. When you reach the main road, turn RIGHT and continue to reach Bynea Railway Station, to catch the train back. *Bynea Station once stood beside sidings which served the Bynea Steel Works and the Yspitty Tin Works.*

reach the clearly indicated Foreshore Car Park. Turn RIGHT here to enter the park. Follow the park road, turning RIGHT when

WALK 15

'A WORLD WITHIN A WORLD OF THE SEA TOWN'

DESCRIPTION *'An ugly, lovely town (or so it was, and is, to me) crawling, sprawling, slummed, unplanned, jerry-villa'd and smug-suburbed by the side of a long and splendid-curving shore where truant boys and sandfield boys and old anonymous men, in the tatters and hangovers of a hundred charity suits, beach combed, idled, and paddled, watched the dock-bound boats, threw stones into the sea for the barking outcast dogs, and, on Saturday summer afternoons, listened to the militant music of salvation and hell-fire preached from a soap-box'...* This was the Swansea of the inimitable poet and playwright Dylan Thomas, the city's most famous son. He was born in 'a Glamorgan villa' in Cwmdonkin Road (visited on this route), and his memory is celebrated in the new centre down by the sea. Today this university city exudes a cosmopolitan air, typified by the extensive marina development explored on this walk. Swansea's latter-day wealth was built upon anthracite and iron ore, but only traces of this industry now remain. This easy walk is about 5 miles long and should take about 3 hours. There are plenty of opportunities to stop, to visit the sights, explore and take refreshment, so be sure to add on the time taken for this.
START Swansea SS657936.

I Leave Swansea Railway Station and walk to the left along the High Street. You reach the ruins of Swansea Castle on the left. Now turn RIGHT into Castle Square. *The water sculpture here reflects upon Dylan Thomas' lines:*

'We sail a boat upon the path, paddle with leaves down an ecstatic line of light'
Dylan Marlais Thomas' (1914-53) unusual middle name derives from the celebrated radical Welsh poet William Thomas, brother of Dylan's paternal grandfather, who wrote as Gwilym Marles. Dylan Thomas married Caitlin in 1937, and later they lived in

Laugharne for a while. Now take the first LEFT into Princess Way. Now continue along Princess Way, and veer to the LEFT into York Street. You come to Victoria Road, which is usually busy with traffic. Cross carefully – there is a central reservation – to reach Cambrian Place and the Swansea Museum. *This museum is Wales' oldest, and still manages to delight visitors with its Egyptian mummy, Swansea and Nantgarw pottery and porcelain, 2000 years of local archaeology, a Victorian gallery and much more. Open 10.00-17.00 Tue-Sun & B. Hols.*

2 When you leave the museum turn RIGHT, then take the first LEFT into Adelaide Road, and walk to the end, where you turn RIGHT into Somerset Place. *On the left you will see The Dylan Thomas Centre, a fitting tribute to Swansea's most famous son. During July and August each year the Dylan Thomas Festival is centred here. Open 10.00-17.00 Tue-Sun & B. Hols. There are also special events and performances.* Now turn RIGHT into East Burrows Road and walk to the end, where you turn RIGHT by Pocketts Wharf to continue along Manheim Quay, with the Tawe Basin on your left. *You pass the Pump House on your left, now converted into a pub, and the Dylan Thomas Theatre, with its splendid mural, on the right. On the waterfront, in front of the Pump House, there is a fine seated statue of Dylan Thomas.* Now continue along Victoria Quay, with museum buildings ahead and to your right, and some fine preserved craft moored to your left.

3 Walk along Victoria Quay with its bars and cafés, keeping the marina to your left, and turning LEFT at the end onto Arethusa Quay. Continue ahead, crossing the cobbled Trawler Road towards the sea front. Now turn RIGHT and walk along the seafront, or on the sands if you wish. Continue beside Oystermouth Road, or along the sands, until you reach a footbridge which crosses the road. Cross here and maintain your direction to turn RIGHT along Gorse Lane, between the Patti Pavilion and St Helen's Cricket & Rugby Ground.

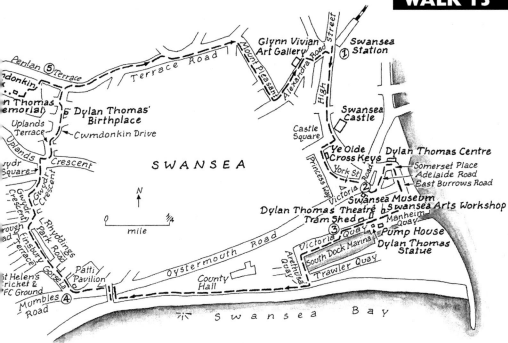

4 Continue ahead, passing the Cricketers pub, to walk up Finsbury Terrace. At the end of this road, turn RIGHT into Marlborough Road, then LEFT into Rhyddings Park Road. Walk ahead into Gwydr Crescent and follow this to the right to Gwydr Square and traffic lights at Uplands Crescent. Turn RIGHT, then very soon LEFT into Uplands Terrace. Walk to the top, and turn RIGHT. After a few yards you will find yourself in Cwmdonkin Drive. *Dylan Thomas' birthplace, at number 5, is near the top, on the right-hand side. It is remarkable only by its association with the great man.* Continue to the end of the road and turn LEFT into Penlan Terrace. Walk along here until you reach an entrance to Cwmdonkin Park on the left. Follow the paths downhill to explore it. *Cwmdonkin Park, built in 1874, was a childhood haunt of Dylan Thomas: 'Though it was only a little park, it held within its borders of old tall trees ... many secret places, caverns and forests, prairies and deserts, as a country somewhere at the end of the sea'. A fenced area encloses the Dylan Thomas Memorial Garden.*

5 Now leave the park the way you came in, and walk back along Penlan Crescent, with fine views of the harbour and the bay ahead and to your right. Pass through a pedestrian barrier in a narrow part of the road and continue ahead. You are now in Terrace Road. Continue ahead along Mount Pleasant. Pass Swansea Institute on your left. When you descend to the main road, turn LEFT. Soon you reach Alexandra Road, with the Glynn Vivian Art Gallery on the left. *Glynn Vivian was the fourth son of John Henry Vivian, owner of the largest copper works in Swansea. The collection is suitably eclectic, with paintings and prints merged with Toby jugs and glass paperweights. There are European and Oriental ceramics, and some fine grandfather clocks. The small garden contains sculpture, and there are visiting exhibitions. Open 10.00-17.00 Tue-Sun & B. Hols.* Now continue along Alexandra Road to return to Swansea Railway Station.

Extracts from *Reminiscences of Childhood*, *Rain Cuts the Place We Tread* and *Fern Hill*, all by Dylan Thomas, are reproduced by kind permission of the publisher, Dent.

The Heart of Wales Line

I f you are travelling along this line for the first time, you will be impressed. Seasoned travellers will need no reminding of the rugged beauty, tranquil villages and picturesque Victorian spa towns that are dotted along one of the most scenic lines in the United Kingdom.

For 121 miles between Shrewsbury and Swansea a feast of panoramic views includes the remote borderlands of the English Marches, the Radnor Forest between Knighton and Llandrindod Wells, red kites in the skies above the Eppynt hills near Llanwrtyd Wells, the meandering River Tywi between Llandovery and Llandeilo, and the beautiful Loughor estuary near Llanelli.

The impressive viaducts at Knucklas and Cynghordy are two of the seven bridges crossed on a journey which also includes six tunnels, and rises to 980 feet above sea level.

The Heart of Wales Line Forum is a consortium of local authorities, the railway industry, the Welsh Development Agency, tourism bodies and the Travellers Association, all committed to the retention and development of the Heart of Wales Railway Line.

KEY TO THE MAPS

- **— ➤** Walk route and direction
- **==** Metalled road
- **- - -** Unsurfaced road
- **• • • •** Footpath/route adjoining walk route
- **~~➔** River/stream
- **⚘ ♧** Trees
- **▰▰▰** Railway
- **G** Gate
- **S** Stile
- **F.B.** Footbridge
- **⥮** Viewpoint
- **P** Parking

THE COUNTRY CODE

- Be safe – plan ahead and follow any signs
- Leave gates and property as you find them
- Protect plants and animals, and take your litter home
- Keep dogs under close control
- Consider other people

The CRoW Act 2000, implemented throughout Wales in May 2005, introduced new legal rights of access for walkers to designated open country, predominantly mountain, moor, heath or down, plus all registered common land. This access can be subject to restrictions and closure for land management or safety reasons for up to 28 days a year.

Published by
Kittiwake 3 Glantwymyn Village Workshops, Machynlleth, Montgomeryshire SY20 8LY

© Text: Heart of Wales Line Forum 2003
© Maps: Morag Perrott 2003

Cover Pictures: *Main* – Knucklas Viaduct; *inset* – Llandrindod Station: David Perrott
First edition 2003; reprints 2007, 2008, 2009 & 2010. Revised edition 2011.

Printed by MWL, Pontypool.

ISBN: **978 1 902302 94 2**